Learning About Birds

By
DEBBIE ROUTH

COPYRIGHT © 2002 Mark Twain Media, Inc.

ISBN 1-58037-189-2

Printing No. CD-1535

Mark Twain Media, Inc., Publishers
Distributed by Carson-Dellosa Publishing Company, Inc.

Table of Contents

Introduction 1

What Are Birds? 2

The History of Birds 4

Birds, Inside-Out: The Anatomy of a Bird 7

Fly, Fly Away 9

Feathers and Flight 12

Parts of a Feather: Student Lab Challenge 15

Classification of Birds 17

Kinds of Birds: Taxonomy 19

A Special Group: Flightless Birds 22

Beaks and Feet: Investigating Bird Adaptations 24

Who's Who: Classification Activity 26

Owl Pellets: Lab Investigation 27

The Behaviors of Birds 29

Migration: Instinctive Seasonal Movement of Animals 33

What Is Ecology? 37

Avian Endangerment Exhibit: Research Project 39

Birds Vocabulary: Study Sheet 40

Birds: Crossword Puzzle 41

Birds: Unit Test 42

Answer Keys 44

Bibliography 46

Introduction

Welcome to a series of books devoted to the *Chordata Phylum*. A **chordate** is an animal that has a spinal cord and vertebrae (backbone). Most chordates have specialized body systems and paired appendages; all at some time in their development have a notochord, dorsal nerve cord, and gill slits. Every animal in the animal kingdom has been subdivided into two main groups, **invertebrates** (without backbone) and **vertebrates** (with backbone). The invertebrates make up 95 percent of the animal kingdom, while vertebrates make up only five percent. The vertebrates are then divided into seven groups called classes: jawless fish, cartilaginous fish, bony fish, amphibians, reptiles, birds, and mammals. Each **class** (group) has special characteristics all its own. This book is devoted to the class of animals called **Aves** (birds).

Birds are easily seen by people and have become important in religion and folklore. Most people have an interest in birds to some degree. They are important economically, providing both food and products made from their feathers and other parts. Shooting birds has provided many with recreation. The simple joy of birdwatching has also become a popular sport. Many people enjoy watching birds because it is a simple pastime. Birds have also proven to be important to us in biological knowledge. Birds, by their health and well-being, can warn us of dangers in our environment.

Birds live in various habitats and are a diversified class of vertebrates. They are varied in their structures because they must be well-suited for the environments in which they live, or they would not be able to survive. Like each group of animals, birds still have many traits or characteristics they share in common with all other birds. Birds are **endothermic** (warm-blooded) vertebrates that have wings and feathers.

Student observers will use many scientific process skills to learn about and appreciate the fascinating world of birds. Students will learn about the origins of birds, their habitats and behaviors, and gain an appreciation of their natural environments. The reinforcement sheets that follow the lessons contain at least one higher-level thinking question. Students will gain a greater interest in science by increasing their ability to practice various scientific skills. Students will observe, classify, analyze, debate, design, and report as they make discoveries about birds and the complex world in which they live.

* Teacher Note: Each lesson opens with a manageable amount of text for the student to read. The succeeding pages contain exercises and illustrations that are plentiful and varied. The lessons may be used as a complete unit for the entire class or as supplemental material. The tone of the book is informal; a dialogue is established between the book and the student.

What Are Birds?

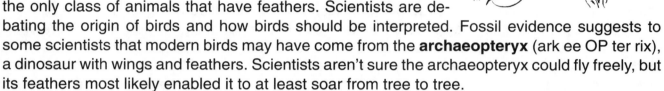

Kingdom: *Animalia*
   Phylum: *Chordata*
      Subphylum: *Vertebrata*
         Class: *Aves* (A veez) means "birds"

Birds are a class of vertebrates that are more complex than reptiles but less complex than mammals. Birds belong to the only class of animals that have feathers. Scientists are debating the origin of birds and how birds should be interpreted. Fossil evidence suggests to some scientists that modern birds may have come from the **archaeopteryx** (ark ee OP ter rix), a dinosaur with wings and feathers. Scientists aren't sure the archaeopteryx could fly freely, but its feathers most likely enabled it to at least soar from tree to tree.

Scientists have named over 9,000 different species of birds. Some live in forests, others live in grasslands, in deserts, on mountaintops, and on uninhabited islands. Since they are warm-blooded (able to maintain a constant body temperature regardless of their surroundings), they can live in very hot or very cold climates. Birds are easy to recognize because they are the only animals with feathers; however, not all birds can fly.

Birds have characteristics that make them well-suited for both flight and life on land. They are warm-blooded vertebrates with wings and feathers, but they also have other characteristics. All birds have beaks (without teeth) that are designed to help them obtain food. They reproduce by laying and incubating fertilized amniotic eggs with hard shells. They are strongly social, as one or both parents provide care for the helpless offspring. Birds also have lightweight, hollow bones that make up their skeletons.

All birds are classified into the class *Aves*. They are then classified even further into five different groups, based on their beaks and **talons** (feet). Bird beaks and talons are modified according to their habitats and the types of food they eat. For example, water birds need webbed feet and a straining beak.

2

Name: _____ Date: _____

What Are Birds?: *Reinforcement Activity*

To the student observer: When you think of birds, do you immediately think of an animal that can fly? Would this be true?

_____

_____

Analyze: Birds of prey are those who hunt other animals for food. Do you think webbed feet would be an advantage or disadvantage for this kind of bird? Why?

_____

_____

1. Solve the puzzle below:

    B ___ ___ ___ ___   Birds have _____ instead of teeth.

    ___ I ___ ___   A vertebrate with wings and feathers.

    ___ ___ R ___ - ___ ___ ___ ___ ___ ___ ___   Birds are _____.

    ___ ___ ___ D ___ ___ ___ ___   Fossil _____ suggests birds came from reptiles.

    ___ ___ ___ ___ S   Birds have _____ instead of arms.

Carefully answer the following.

2. Name two adaptations of birds for flight. _____

    _____

3. Some scientists believe _____ may be the ancestors of birds.

4. Birds are more complex than _____ but less complex than

    _____.

5. Birds are members of the class _____.

6. List five main characteristics of birds.

    a. _____

    b. _____

    c. _____

    d. _____

    e. _____

The History of Birds

Class Aves

Birds, as you've already learned, are animals in the class *Aves.* They are the most beautiful and observable members of the animal kingdom. Birds are different from other animals, because they have hollow bones and feathers. The members of this class are extremely **diversified** (varied). They range in size from 6 cm (a species of hummingbird) to 2.5 m (the ostrich). Since birds are **endothermic** (warm-blooded) and can fly, they can be found living on every continent in every habitat.

Ornithology

The study of birds is very popular. People have always had a fascination with them. Birds have been symbolic throughout time to people of all cultures and religions. Many birdwatchers consider themselves to be **ornithologists**. An ornithologist is someone who studies birds, their origins, their behaviors, and their roles in the biosphere. You might even become a serious birdwatcher yourself after completing this unit!

The Origin of Birds

Some scientists believe reptiles may be the ancestors of birds. Fossils show a link between reptiles and birds. However, fossil records are fragmented and incomplete because birds' feathers and fragile bones do not fossilize well.

Archaeopteryx (Means "Ancient Wing")

The earliest well-preserved fossil known to have feathers is archaeopteryx. Many scientists consider this the first bird. Archaeopteryx had several reptilian features: teeth, a head covered in scales, claws (even on its wings), and a bony tail. Although this early bird was probably only able to glide, not fly, it is very similar to some of the birds we know today.

Hesperornis and Ichthyornis: "A Couple of Early Birds"

These two fossils, **hesperornis** (western bird) and **ichthyornis** (fish bird), were found after archaeopteryx. Hesperornis, a large loon-like flightless bird, had teeth and legs modified for swimming. Ichthyornis, a gull-sized bird, was probably a good flier with well-formed wings. New fossil remains continue to be discovered as **paleontologists** (people who study fossils) continue to seek answers regarding the origin of birds.

Name: _____ Date: _____

The History of Birds: *Reinforcement Activity*

To the student observer: Can you summarize the differences between birds and the other vertebrate animals?

_____

_____

_____

Analyze: Why do you think feathers and hollow bones do not fossilize well?

_____

_____

Directions: Complete the following questions below.

1. What are two characteristics that distinguish birds from the other vertebrates? _____

   _____

   _____

2. What is ornithology? _____

   _____

3. Birds belong to what class? _____

4. Why do some scientists believe reptiles may be the ancestors of birds? _____

   _____

   _____

   _____

5. Who are paleontologists? _____

   _____

6. What reptilian characteristics can you identify from the illustration of the archaeopteryx on the next page?

   _____

   _____

   _____

   _____

Name: _____ Date: _____

The History of Birds: *Reinforcement Activity (cont.)*

ARCHAEOPTERYX—THE FIRST BIRD

Birds, Inside-Out: *The Anatomy of a Bird*

The outer surface of a bird's body, except for its bill and feet, is usually covered with feathers. Feathers cover the bird's wings and body and help keep it warm by providing insulation. Some birds, such as the vulture, have bare heads and necks. Another bird, the bald eagle, isn't really bald at all. It has plenty of white feathers on its head and neck. Birds are the only vertebrate animals capable of true powered flight. The wings of a bird are shaped very much like the wings of a plane. They are curved from the front to the back, creating lift for flight. Birds have thin skin and scales on their legs and feet. Birds have small, covered ear openings and a keen sense of hearing.

Inside the streamlined, elongated body of the bird, there is a unique skeletal and muscular system. The skull is joined to the backbone by bony vertebrae, and the internal organs are protected by a rib cage as in all vertebrates. The bird's skeleton has been modified for flight. The bones are hollow and lightweight but are fused together for strength. The bone structure of larger birds has a crisscross network of struts that strengthens the hollow center. The huge eye sockets and toothless beak reduce the weight of the skull. A bird has a long neck that enables it to catch food and to reach all parts of its body. The bird's neck has more bones than the other vertebrates. The wishbone, or clavicle, supports the massive **pectoral** (chest) muscles. Although the skeleton is light, the muscles are large and heavy. The pectoral muscles make up 25 percent of a bird's body weight and are used to move the wings. Much of the space inside the bird's body is taken up by air sacs that are connected to the lungs. The air sacs move up into the neck, upper wing bones, lungs, chest, and abdomen.

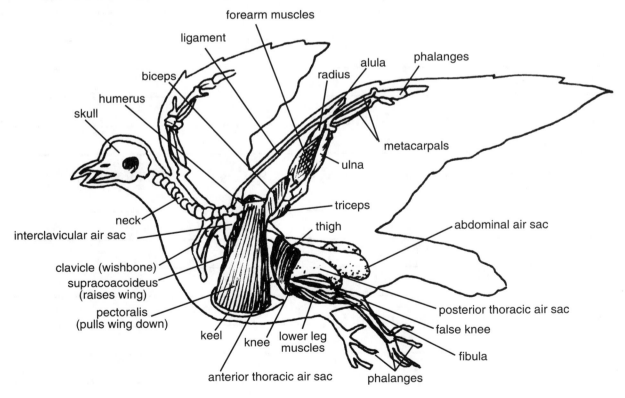

Name: _____ Date: _____

Birds, Inside-Out: *Reinforcement Activity*

To the student observer: Do you know why feathers are so important? _____

_____

_____

_____

Analyze: What reptilian characteristic is still present in modern birds? _____

_____

Directions: Complete the following questions.

1. Describe how a bird's skeleton is modified for flight. _____

   _____

   _____

   _____

   _____

2. Describe how the wings of a bird are designed for true flight. _____

   _____

   _____

   _____

   _____

3. What is the largest muscle in a bird's body? _____

   _____

4. What takes up most of the space in a bird's body? How is this helpful to a bird?

   _____

   _____

   _____

   _____

5. How is a bird's head designed for flight? _____

   _____

   _____

   _____

Fly, Fly Away

Birds Are Built for Flight

Flight requires a tremendous amount of energy; a light, strong skeleton; wings; and feathers. A bird's entire body is adapted for flight. Some of the adaptations it has for flight are internal. Let's take a close look at the bird's many structures for flight.

Wings

The bones in a bird's wing are very much like a human arm. A bird has a shoulder, an upper arm and elbow, a lower arm and wrist, and a hand with fingers and a thumb. However, our hand is different from a bird's hand. We have more bones and fingers, and we can move all our fingers. A bird has a narrow hand with only two fingers that are joined together so they can't move. Birds can only move their thumbs.

The shape of a bird's wing is one way birds are built for flight. The wing is slightly curved from front to back and is thicker in the front. This allows the air to flow faster above the wing than below it. The difference in air speeds provides the lift.

A Lightweight Body

Beneath the feathers, a bird's body is quite small. It is designed to weigh as little as possible. Inside the body are bubble-like structures filled with air. These air sacs, which are attached to the lungs, spread throughout a bird's body and into its bones. The air sacs help to cool the body and lessen its weight. The body of a bird is compact and has a contoured shape.

Birds have hollow bones that are fused together; this eliminates the need for heavy ligaments. The air sacs inside the bones make them lighter in weight by reducing bone density. Even though a bird's bones are hollow, they are not brittle and weak. In fact, they are very strong due to the cross braces or struts inside them.

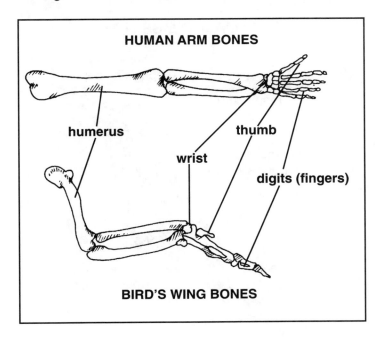

HUMAN ARM BONES

humerus

thumb

wrist

digits (fingers)

BIRD'S WING BONES

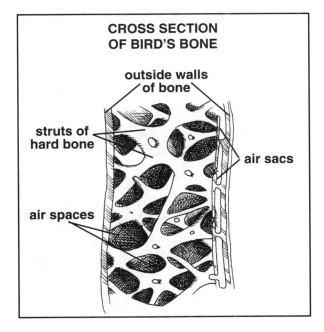

CROSS SECTION
OF BIRD'S BONE

outside walls
of bone

struts of
hard bone

air sacs

air spaces

Fly, Fly Away (cont.)

Energy

Birds obtain the energy they need for flying from the food they eat. Birds eat large amounts of food and have an efficient digestive system that breaks down food quickly. Quick digestion enables the bird to have constant energy. Birds also have efficient circulatory and respiratory systems that keep their energy levels high and their weights low.

Feathers

Flight feathers must be strong enough to bend without breaking, yet light enough to float in a breeze. Feathers need to lie flat so the air slides over them and the body tapers smoothly from beak to tail. Birds fold their legs in tightly against their bodies, and even their ears are hidden beneath head feathers. The flight feathers are anchored to the wing bones. The longest feathers for flight are called **primaries** and are attached to the hand section. Attached to the lower arm bones are the **secondaries**. The secondaries are a little shorter than the primaries. The **tertiaries** (TER she air eez) are the other feathers that close the gap between the elbow and the shoulder.

Muscles

Flight muscles are attached to the **keel**, or breastbone. The outer set of muscles lowers the wings, while the inner set raises them. The lowering muscles are the largest because the bird must work its hardest to pull its wings down. A bird's body has large, heavy muscles. The pectoral muscles that move the wings make up 25 percent of a bird's body weight.

WING FLIGHT FEATHERS

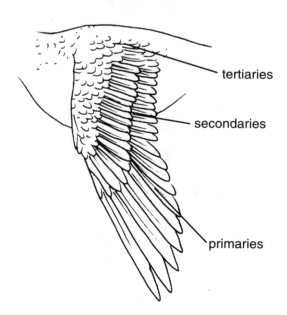

tertiaries

secondaries

primaries

MAJOR MUSCLES

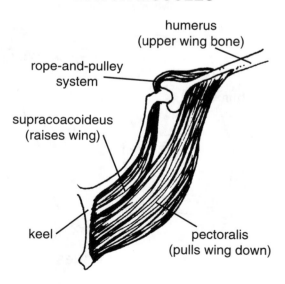

humerus (upper wing bone)

rope-and-pulley system

supracoacoideus (raises wing)

keel

pectoralis (pulls wing down)

Name: _____ Date: _____

Fly, Fly Away: *Reinforcement Activity*

To the student observer: How do the wings of a bird resemble your arm?

_____

_____

_____

Directions: Describe below how birds are built for flight.

1. Wings _____

   _____

   _____

   _____

2. Body _____

   _____

   _____

   _____

3. Feathers _____

   _____

   _____

   _____

4. Muscles _____

   _____

   _____

5. Energy _____

   _____

   _____

Feathers and Flight

Feathers are the special body coverings that define a bird. This wonderful development separates birds from all other animals. At first, a feather closely resembles a reptile's scale. After it begins to grow and develop, the feather branches out and changes into fluffy heat-conserving insulation. It continues to grow and develop into a complex structure with special-ized functions.

Important Functions

The feathers have four important functions. Feathers provide insulation to pro-tect the bird from cold weather. Feathers are helpful in the miracle of flight. They create the wing and tail surfaces that are necessary for flight. They waterproof the bird's body through the act of **preening** (a bird's ability to rub oil onto its feathers). Feathers also provide coloration for camouflage from enemies and courtship dis-plays to help them attract a mate. Color and patterns aid in the identification of birds; often, a single feather is sufficient to identify a bird.

Two Main Types

The contour feather and the down feather are the two main types of bird feathers. The **contour feathers** are the **pennae**, or outer feathers, that give birds their coloring and smooth, sleek shape. These are also the feathers a bird uses for flight. The body feathers streamline the bird's body. The flight feathers are those that extend beyond the body. Flight feathers are the tail and wing feathers. The tail feathers are used for steering, balance, and display. The wing feathers are the strongest feathers and are shaped to provide the power for flight. The shape of a bird's wing is similar to the shape of an airplane wing. The wing is slightly curved from the front to the back and thicker in the front. The wing feath-ers smooth the airflow over the wing while decreasing the air pressure above the wing and providing the lift needed for flight.

Contour feather

The **down feathers** are the **plumulae** or inner feathers that are soft, finely-divided feathers used to help the bird stay warm. The down feathers trap a layer of air to provide insulation. The down feather is fluffy because the **barbules** (threadlike parts fringing each side of the barbs of a feather) are arranged randomly and have no hooks to lock the feathers together like contour feathers. Down feathers are the feathers that cover the bodies of most young birds.

Down feathers

Structure

Feathers are made of a protein called **keratin**. Keratin gives feathers great strength and flexibility. As feathers develop and become fully grown, their blood supply is cut off, and the feather is no longer living. The bird keeps the nonliving feather until it becomes worn-out. The worn-out feather is replaced as it falls off or is pushed out by a new feather. This process is called **molting** (shedding) the old feather and growing a new one.

Feathers and Flight (cont.)

Parts of a Feather

Contour feathers have a **vane** (the flat part of the feather that includes the barbs) and a central **shaft** full of air pockets. Protruding out from the shaft are many branches called **barbs**. Each barb is made up of hundreds of interlocking **barbules**. Barbules lock together to form a continuous surface that allows air to flow over. They lie on either side of each barb, forming hooks and catches. If a barbule hook comes loose, a bird preens it back into position with its beak. A down feather has a shorter shaft with tufts of long, fluffy barbules, and it does not interlock.

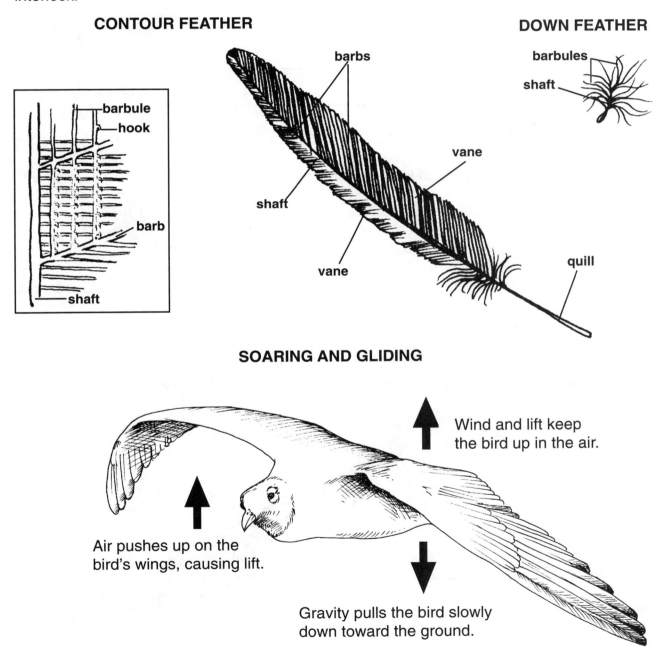

CONTOUR FEATHER

barbs

barbule

hook

barb

shaft

shaft

vane

vane

quill

DOWN FEATHER

barbules

shaft

SOARING AND GLIDING

Wind and lift keep the bird up in the air.

Air pushes up on the bird's wings, causing lift.

Gravity pulls the bird slowly down toward the ground.

Name: _____ Date: _____

Feathers and Flight: *Reinforcement Activity*

To the student observer: Do you know what body covering birds have that make them different from all other animals?

_____

Directions: Complete the questions below.

1. State four functions of feathers.

    a. _____

    b. _____

    c. _____

    d. _____

2. What are the two main types of feathers and their purposes?

    a. _____

    b. _____

3. What are feathers made of? _____

_____

4. Label the parts of the feather below. (Some words may be used more than once.)

    barb   **barbule**   **hook**   **quill**   **shaft**

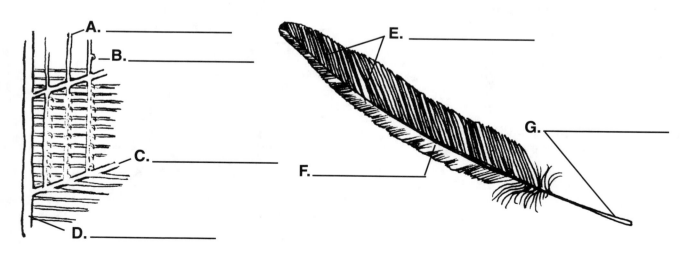

A. _____

B. _____

C. _____

D. _____

E. _____

F. _____

G. _____

Name: _____ Date: _____

Parts of a Feather: *Student Lab Challenge*

To the student observer: Do you know the two main kinds of feathers and their parts? This lab challenge will check your abilities to be able to make observations and diagram while comparing feathers.

Problem: Can you classify and identify the parts of a feather?

Birds have two main kinds of feathers. A body covering of feathers is a special characteristic of birds. **Down feathers** are small and fluffy feathers that lie close to a bird's body. These feathers are very important to a bird. They help to keep the bird warm by providing insulation against the cold and keeping its body temperature constant. While observing down feathers, note how they are adapted for the job they do. **Contour feathers** are large, stiff feathers that cover the whole body, giving the bird color and helping it to fly. Birds also have feathers called **filoplumes**, or pinfeathers. These are long hair-like feathers. Filoplumes grow in groups near contour feathers and help control the movement of the contour feathers.

Materials:
Different feathers from different kinds of birds
A hand lens
Dissecting needle or T-pin
Scissors

Filoplumes   **Contour feather**   **Down feathers**

Procedure:
1. Obtain four different bird feathers from your teacher. Examine each feather with your hand lens carefully. Use the drawings above and from the previous lesson to help you. (Teacher note: make sure each group has at least one contour, one down, and one filoplume feather.)
2. Classify your feathers into three groups. (down, contour, filoplumes)
3. Draw each feather on the observation page and label the quill, shaft, vane, barbs and barbules.
4. Observe the vane of each feather.
5. Look at the barbs. Using a dissecting needle, separate the barbs and look for the barbules that hook the barbs together.
6. Using your hand lens, observe what happens when you slowly pull each feather between your thumb and forefinger. Write your observations here.

_____

_____

_____

7. Cut about 2 cm off the end of the shaft and examine the cut end with your hand lens. Write your observations here.

_____

_____

_____

Name: _____ Date: _____

Parts of a Feather: *Student Lab Challenge (cont.)*

Observations: Draw and label each of your feathers below.

A. Contour feather

B. Down feather

C. Filoplume (Pinfeather)

Conclusions:

1. How is the structure of a contour feather adapted for flight? _____
   _____
   _____

2. How is a down feather adapted for insulation? _____
   _____
   _____

3. Why is pinfeather a proper name for the filoplumes? _____
   _____
   _____

4. Use your own paper to compare the shape, barbs, and shaft of each of the two main types of feathers.

Classification of Birds

Scientists around the world place **organisms** (living things) into groups, which makes it easier to study and learn about them. For example, let's say you need a box of cereal from the grocery store. You know exactly where to look in the store for the different kinds of cereals. This is because the store is **classified** (grouped) by types of food, based on similarities. Bread products, meat products, canned goods, bakery goods, and dairy products are each in their own section of the store. This enables the grocers, as well as the customers, to find things more easily.

Birds, like all living things, are classified into groups. Birds are very diversified and live in almost every type of habitat. There are nearly 9,000 different species of birds. Scientists needed a way to communicate about so many different kinds of birds to avoid errors in communication. Classification is used to make sense of this amazing diversity by grouping related forms together. The groupings are arranged from the most general relationship to the most specific relationship. They are grouped and then regrouped over and over, until the only organism left in the group is one of a kind. The seven levels of classification include kingdom, phylum, class, order, family, genus, and species.

The science of classification is called **taxonomy**. The best way to understand taxonomy is by looking at a specific bird and following it through the system. The blackheaded gull is classified as follows:

Level	Characteristics
Kingdom - *Animalia*	• multicellular, moves about, can't make its own food
Phylum - *Chordata*	• has a backbone
Class - *Aves*	• an animal that has feathers
Order - *Charandriformes*	• wader-like ancestor, all have long legs, webbed feet, and heavy bill
Family - *Laridae*	• efficient fliers
Genus - *Larus*	• shallow-water birds found near the coastlines
Species - *ridibundus*	• small birds with slender bills; have a brown hood during mating season

Blackheaded gull during mating season

The genus name and the species name are used together to form the bird's scientific name. The scientific name for the blackheaded gull is *Larus ridibundus*. Scientific names are based on the ancient language of Latin, a language that scientists use. The genus name is always capitalized, and the species name is not. The scientific name is always italicized. Carolus Linnaeus developed this two-word naming system called **binomial nomenclature**. This enables scientists to give specific names to living things, avoiding confusion with their more common names.

17

Classification of Birds: *Reinforcement Activity*

To the student observer: What is the purpose of classification? _____

_____

Analyze: Why do you think it is important for all living things to have a scientific name?

_____

_____

Directions: Answer the following questions below.

1. How are the classification levels arranged? _____

   _____

   _____

2. What is the name for the science of classification? _____

   _____

3. What level clearly identifies the blackheaded gull as a bird? _____

4. At what level is it identified as a wading bird? _____

5. At what level is it identified as a blackheaded gull? _____

6. Who developed the classification system we use today? _____

7. What is the classification system called? _____

8. Number the seven classification levels in order, with "1" being the first, most general level and "7" being the last, most specific level.
   - _____ A. Class
   - _____ B. Family
   - _____ C. Order
   - _____ D. Species
   - _____ E. Phylum
   - _____ F. Kingdom
   - _____ G. Genus

Kinds of Birds: *Taxonomy*

Birds are difficult for scientists to classify because of their numbers and diversity. Scientists group birds according to their body structure, beak structure, foot structure, behavior, and song. Aves are divided into 27 different orders. The largest order is made up of the perching songbirds. Perching songbirds make up 60 percent of the **avian** (bird) species. The smallest order, the grebes, make up an order of their own. Most taxonomists agree that there are five main groups of birds. Taxonomists use the structure of the beaks and feet to place a bird into one of these groups.

Five Main Groups by Beaks and Feet

Group	Beaks	Feet	Examples
Bird of Prey	Tearing	Grasping	Hawk
Perching Bird	Cracking/ Boring	Perching	Cardinal
Nonperching Bird	Chiseling	Clinging	Woodpecker
Wading Bird	Spearing	Wading	Heron
Swimming Bird	Straining	Webbed	Duck

The Birds of Prey

Birds of prey are the most powerful birds. They live by killing and eating other animals. Birds of prey have hooked beaks and large feet with strong curving **talons** (claws). The beak is designed for tearing flesh and is sometimes used for killing. The talons are long and curved for capturing and grasping onto prey. Birds of prey seize their prey with their feet as they swoop down from the air. They have two toes that face forward and two toes that face backward. These hunters come in all sizes. Eagles are the largest birds of prey. Falconets and pygmy owls weigh less than 60 g (2 oz.), making them the smallest birds of prey. Birds of prey are found almost all over the world, in all types of habitats. There are two groups of birds of prey: the **diurnal** hunters that hunt by day and the **nocturnal** hunters that hunt by night. Birds of prey have very keen eyesight. They see eight times better than humans do.

The Perching Birds

There are two groups of perching birds: insect-eaters and seed-eaters. Perching birds make up the largest group of birds. Over half of all birds fall into this division. There are aerial insect-eaters, such as swallows and nuthatches. The heavy-billed seed-eaters include finches and sparrows. Other perching birds include the many songbirds, such as cardinals, bluebirds, robins, juncos, and orioles. Their beaks or bills are designed for the type of food they eat. If they eat seeds and fruit, they have strong, broad bills that will crack the seeds and a rough tongue designed to clean out the seed. If they eat insects, the bill is designed to bore into wood to find insects within. The most notable feature is the perching foot—three toes point forward and one points backward.

Kinds of Birds: *Taxonomy (cont.)*

The Nonperching Land Birds

Nonperching land birds are tree- or ground-dwelling birds that feed on seeds and fruit. Including nearly 300 species, the group is dominated by the doves and pigeons. Doves and pigeons produce a milky substance to feed their young. They are fast, strong fliers and thrive in their contact with humans. The woodpecker is often placed in this division. Woodpeckers have special beaks and thick skulls that are designed for hammering into wood. These birds have strong toes for clinging to the trees and tails to brace their bodies. Also at home on the ground are many game birds, such as pheasants and quails. These birds prefer to walk rather than fly. They rely heavily on their ability to camouflage themselves to avoid being detected. They live in almost every habitat and feed mainly on fruit and seeds that have fallen to the ground.

The Water Birds: Swimming and Wading Birds

Most water birds feed on the surface of the water; however, a few species dive for fish and mollusks. Sometimes these birds stir the water up with their feet and filter through the shallow bottom sediments; sometimes they graze on land for food.

Swimming birds include loons, penguins, ducks, and geese. Waterfowl such as ducks, geese, and swans have bills that are flat, broad, and somewhat rounded at the tip. These migratory birds are distributed worldwide and feed on aquatic plants and animals. They use their strong thighs and webbed feet to streak through the water. A loon is very similar to a duck, except the beak or bill is not as flat or rounded. Loons are diving birds that live in the Northern Hemisphere. The loon's legs are set so far back on its body that walking on land is very difficult; it appears to be very clumsy. Penguins are another group of diving birds. They live in the cold oceans of the Southern Hemisphere. Their most notable trait is their modified wings that they use as flippers; however, the wings are useless for flight. Penguins have insulating feathers and a dense layer of fat for protection from the frigid waters.

Wading birds include the herons, flamingos, storks, and ibises. All are long-legged and live in or near shallow water. They eat fish, crustaceans, mollusks, small mammals, other birds, and insects. The flamingo filters algae and invertebrates by using its down-bent bill and fleshy tongue. The herons form the largest group of water birds. The heron is a slender, long-necked bird that catches its supper with its dagger-like bill. It is easy to recognize in flight—it flies long distances with a bent "s-shaped" neck and its long legs stretched out far behind it. Storks are capable of soaring flight and feed on animal matter. The ibises and spoonbills make up another division of wading birds that live in the tropical climates. The ibises have long, downward-curved bills, and spoonbills have flattened bills with a spoon-like tip.

Kinds of Birds: *Taxonomy (cont.)*

Bird of Prey

Wading Bird

Swimming Bird

Perching Bird

Nonperching Land Bird

A Special Group: *Flightless Birds*

While flight is the usual form of movement used by most birds, they also use other methods to move around. The flightless birds use their legs to run or swim; they fall into two main groups: ostriches and penguins. The flightless birds all have one characteristic in common—they have reduced wings and flight muscles and have lost their ability to fly. There is a theory that at one time food shortage made them unable to obtain enough food for the energy needed for flight. A bird that doesn't fly requires less food and has a better chance of surviving. The huge muscles necessary for flight were not being used, so they reduced in size. The large birds developed huge, strong legs for running and became too heavy to fly. The adapted trait was then passed down to their offspring. Of course, this is just a theory.

Penguins

Penguins live in the Antarctic and are marine birds, more comfortable in the water than on land. They are ideally adapted for diving. There are 18 living species of penguins. Penguins feed on fish, squid, and crustaceans found underwater. Since their food supply is abundant only in the water, swimming is much more beneficial to them than flying. They have modified wings that function as flippers. They have short feathers and a heavy layer of fat to protect them from the cold waters they inhabit. Penguins use their short legs to march upright in a line one by one; or sometimes they slide quite rapidly across the ice on their stomachs as if on a sled. Wouldn't that be fun?

Ostriches and Other Ratites

Ratite is a term used by taxonomists to identify several orders of large, flightless birds. The word *ratites* refers to the flat shape of the sternum, which lacks the keel shape of flying birds. This group of birds includes the emu, rhea, cassowary, kiwi, and ostrich. Ratites all have powerful legs, and most are excellent runners. Most species except the kiwi, feed on plant material. A kiwi uses its long bill to capture earthworms and insects from the forest floor. Ostriches live in the dry plains of Arabia and Africa. They can weigh up to 200 pounds and stand up to eight feet tall. The ostrich is the largest bird and can run as fast as a horse.

Name: _____ Date: _____

Kinds of Birds: *Reinforcement Activity*

To the student observer: Why are birds difficult to classify? _____

_____

_____

Analyze: How do scientists group birds? _____

_____

_____

Directions: Answer the following questions.

1. What are the five main groups of birds, classified by beaks and feet?

    a. _____

    b. _____

    c. _____

    d. _____

    e. _____

2. Which group of birds is the largest group? _____

3. What is the largest bird of prey? _____

4. Name two groups of flightless birds.

    a. _____

    b. _____

5. What characteristic is common among all flightless birds? _____

    _____

Matching

_____ 6.   Long-legged birds   A. Birds of prey

_____ 7.   Tree- or ground-dwellers   B. Perching birds

_____ 8.   Waterfowl   C. Nonperching birds

_____ 9.   Powerful hunters   D. Wading birds

_____ 10. Songbirds   E. Swimming birds

Name: _____ Date: _____

Beaks and Feet: *Investigating Bird Adaptations*

To the student observer: Adaptations are the traits of a living thing that help it survive in its habitat. Can you match the correct foot and beak adaptations below and on the next page?

Feet

Directions: Place the letter of the type of foot at the bottom of the page next to its description below.

Types of feet: **swimming   perching   wading   clinging   grasping**

_____ 1.   Foot adapted to swimming (webbed)

_____ 2.   Foot adapted to catching and killing prey (strong curved talons for grasping)

_____ 3.   Foot adapted to clamp around a branch (three toes face forward, and one toe faces backward)

_____ 4.   Foot adapted for clinging or climbing (curved talons; two toes face forward, and two toes face backward)

_____ 5.   Foot adapted to wading through shallow waters (long toes and long legs)

A.

B.
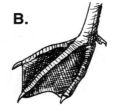

C.

D.

E.

24

Name: _____ Date: _____

Beaks and Feet: *Investigating Bird Adaptations (cont.)*

Beaks

Directions: Place the letter of the type of beak at the bottom of the page next to its description below.

Types of beaks: **spearing   cracking   straining   chisel   spoon   probing   tearing**

_____ 1.   Beak adapted to cracking hard seed shells (cracking)

_____ 2.   Beak adapted for spearing fish from shallow waters (spearing)

_____ 3.   Beak adapted for digging insects out of wood (chisel)

_____ 4.   Beak adapted for straining mud from plants and shellfish (straining)

_____ 5.   Beak adapted for gathering vegetation and small aquatic animals from lakes (spoon)

_____ 6.   Beak adapted for tearing meat (tearing)

_____ 7.   Beak adapted for probing insects (probing)

A.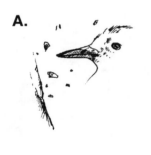

B.

C.

D.

E.

F.

G.

Name: _____ Date: _____

Who's Who: *Classification Activity*

To the student observer: Classify each of the birds below as one of the following: **perching bird**, **nonperching bird**, **bird of prey**, **wading bird**, **swimming bird**, or **flightless bird**.

A. _____

B. _____

C. _____

D. _____

E. _____

F. _____

G. _____

H. _____

Name: _____ Date: _____

Owl Pellets: *Lab Investigation*

To the student observer: Birds of prey generally swallow their prey whole. The digestive system cannot dissolve bones, feathers, or hair. The remains form a ball in the bird's stomach. These balls seem to be important for proper digestion but no one knows how these balls form. The bird later regurgitates the undigested material, called **balls of rejection**. Many of these balls are found under the birds' nests or in the general area. Ornithologists study the balls of rejection to learn about the diet of birds.

Problem: What does an owl eat?

Materials needed per group:

Owl pellet   Dissecting needle
Metric ruler   Optional—rubber gloves
Hand lens

Procedure:
1. Obtain an owl pellet from your teacher and observe the external characteristics with your hand lens. Record your observations.
2. Gently break the pellet into two parts.
3. Use your dissecting needle to separate any undigested material from the pellet. Remove all fur from any skulls you find.
4. Group bones together into similar groups
5. Observe all skull bones and record data from your observations. Record the number, length, shape, and the color of the teeth.
6. Try to determine the kind of skulls present from the table below.
7. Try fitting together the bones to form complete skeletons.

Table:

Prey	Skull Characteristics
Mole	Upper jaw has 18 teeth or more. Skull length is 23 mm or more.
Meadow Vole	Upper jaw has two biting teeth. Molars are flat and jaws are even in front.
Mouse	Upper jaw has two biting teeth and extends past lower jaw. Skull length is 22 mm or less.
Rat	Upper jaw has two biting teeth and extends past lower jaw. Skull length is 23 mm or more.
Shrew	Upper jaw has 18 brown teeth or more. Skull length is 23 mm or less.

Name: _____   Date: _____

Owl Pellets: *Lab Investigation (cont.)*

Observations:

1. Describe what an owl pellet looks like. _____

   _____

   _____

   _____

   _____

2. What kind of bones did you find to be most numerous? _____

   _____

3. Did some of the bones appear to be missing as you tried to construct a skeleton? If so, why do you think some of them were missing?

   _____

   _____

   _____

   _____

Conclusions:

4. What kind of animals do you think the owl ate most frequently? What evidence supports your answer?

   _____

   _____

   _____

5. Why do owls regurgitate or cough up pellets? _____

   _____

   _____

   _____

6. What characteristics do owls have that help them eat and capture their prey?

   _____

   _____

   _____

   _____

The Behaviors of Birds

Survival

A bird, like all living things in the animal kingdom, has survival as its main objective. Birds display some of the most complex animal behaviors as they respond to their environments. Living things respond to stimuli in different ways. A **stimulus** is anything in the environment that causes a response. The way an **organism** (living thing) responds to stimuli is called **behavior**. Behavior is the way an organism acts. There are two forms of behavior demonstrated by organisms: innate behavior and acquired or learned behavior. A behavior an organism is born with is called **innate** behavior. Innate behaviors can be **reflex** or **instinct**. A reflex act does not involve the brain; it is an automatic response. Instincts are more complex, as the brain is involved in these behaviors. Nest building and migration are two examples of instinctive behaviors in most birds. Birds do not have to be shown how to build nests. A behavior that is learned is called **acquired** or **learned** behavior. Birds have acquired many learned behaviors, such as learning where food is likely to be found.

Song and Territoriality

Staking Their Claim

The songs of birds may be inherited, but the bird must practice to sing it perfectly. Singing is directed at other birds of the same species to communicate a message. Songs announce a bird's presence and its rank in the pecking order. Song increases to attract a mate during breeding season or to protect a territory. A bird's song demonstrates the fitness of a male as a suitable mate and warns competing males to stay away.

Birds need a space to live. The space in which they live is called a **territory**. The territory includes a food supply and a suitable nesting site well hidden from predators. Territories are protected with song and visual displays. Birds will also defend this area with force, if necessary. Watch your bird feeders in the spring, and you will see birds staking their claims. A song or call is also helpful when identifying a species of bird.

Courtship

The ways in which birds find partners is one of the most fascinating and colorful features in the animal kingdom. Courtship behavior in birds includes song, dance, aerial displays, posturing, or calls. Before breeding, a male bird marks out an area by singing or dancing. He then has to attract a mate, because most birds do not live in pairs. A few species, such as the Bewick's swan, choose a mate for life. The males may also dance around or show off their fine feathers. A peacock will strut around and show off its fantastic tail feathers. The vigor and skill of a bird's displays indicates his fitness as a mate; however, it is the female who chooses the male. The sequence of courtship behavior begins with territorial defense and song, followed by mate-attraction displays, courtship feeding (the male offers tidbits of food to the female), and the selection of the nesting site. It is important for a bird to find a mate so its genetic traits will be passed on.

The Behaviors of Birds (cont.)

Nesting

     Each kind of bird makes a unique nest. Nests range in size from the thimble-like construction of the hummingbirds to the huge two-ton nest of the eagle. They range in complexity from the meadowlark, which lays her eggs in a hole in the ground made by a horse's hoof, to the intricate woven nest of the orioles. Usually the male selects the nesting site, and the female is the main builder of the nest. The male may help with the building or collecting of the materials. Birds use grass, twigs, man-made materials, animal hair or fur, and mud to build their homes. City birds use twine, tinfoil, paper, and tissue to build their nests. Birds nest anywhere from the ground up to great heights; water birds make floating nests anchored to aquatic plants. Some birds are very social and build a community nest that is shared by many birds. All nests must be large enough to contain the female bird and her **brood** (young). The nests may be very common or very unusual in design or complexity, but any bird building a nest is following an instinctive blueprint that is fascinating to watch.

Feeding

     If it's edible, there is a bird somewhere that eats it. Most birds eat arthropods and vegetation, since these are the two most abundant sources on earth. Birds are generally specialized feeders. Very few birds are omnivores. The various forms of beaks and bills reflect their specialization. Cardinals with their strong cone-shaped beaks are adapted for crushing seeds, but it would be impossible for them to eat a mouse. How birds eat is as interesting as what they eat. **Gleaning** (the act of gathering food, piece by piece) is used by birds as a common method of obtaining food. Birds' methods of acquiring food include ground gleaning, foliage gleaning, bark gleaning, aerial feeding in flight, and aquatic feeding. Hummingbirds specialize in nectar gleaning. Each bird is limited to the type of food it eats, depending on the type of bill it has. Although they may prefer one method of obtaining food, many birds use a combination of these methods. This is especially true of those few who are omnivores.

The Behaviors of Birds (cont.)

Molting

Birds need to shed their old and worn-out feathers. The shedding of these feathers is called **molting**. Molting keeps the bird's plumage looking smooth and healthy; feathers are important to the bird's survival. The old feathers are cast off by the bird and replaced with a quill that will produce a new feather. Most birds molt at least once a year. Sometimes they molt at the end of the mating season. They cast off the bright colors used for mating and replace them with dull ones that will enable them to blend more easily with their surroundings. Sometimes they molt with the seasons. Many birds molt a little at a time so they do not lose all of their primary flight feathers at once. However, ducks, geese, and swans lose their feathers all at once and cannot fly during that time.

Preening

Preening is a process birds use to protect their feathers from rain and water. They do this by rubbing an oil substance from their preening gland onto their feathers with their beaks. The preening gland is located at the base of the tail. The bird uses its beak like a comb to draw together the barbs and barbules. Birds also care for their feathers by **powdering** (when special feathers break down and form a powder) and by bathing in water and dust. Sometimes birds let ants swarm all over them by dusting in an anthill. They do this to drive away **parasites** (organisms that live off a host).

Camouflage and Predation

Birds, like all animals, depend on blending in with their surroundings to avoid being discovered by a predator. For birds that live by feeding and roosting on the ground, survival depends on the ability to blend in with their environments to avoid detection by predators. This is called **camouflage**. The birds that do not fly south for the winter, change their feathers with the seasons to avoid detection from enemies.

For birds of prey, survival depends on the ability to hunt successfully. **Predation** is a behavior of birds of prey that involves a sequence of events. First, the bird must determine a place to hunt that is abundant in food. Next, the bird must search for prey by circling the area until a victim is found. Then, in the final stage, the chase and capture take place. Birds of prey generally swallow their prey whole.

Name: _____ Date: _____

The Behaviors of Birds: *Reinforcement Activity*

To the student observer: What is behavior? _____

_____

Analyze: What is an example of a stimulus you responded to today? _____

_____

Directions: Answer the questions below.

1. What is a stimulus? _____

   _____

   _____

2. What are the two forms of behavior?

   a. _____

   b. _____

3. What are two types of innate behaviors?

   a. _____

   b. _____

Matching

_____ 4. Laying Eggs

_____ 5. Shedding feathers

_____ 6. Protecting feathers from rain

_____ 7. Blending in with the environment

_____ 8. Singing to competing males

_____ 9. Showing off fine feathers

_____ 10. Gathering food

_____ 11. Circling an area for prey

A. Preening

B. Molting

C. Gleaning

D. Camouflage

E. Predation

F. Nesting

G. Courtship

H. Territoriality

Migration: *Instinctive Seasonal Movement of Animals*

One of the most amazing of all the bird behaviors is **migration**. Approximately half of the species of birds on Earth migrate. Migration can be a long annual journey in flocks, or a solitary biannual trip up or down a mountain. Some birds do not need to migrate; they remain in their normal habitat throughout the year. Scientists are still studying the question of how birds navigate to find their way over such long distances.

Why Do Birds Migrate?

Like all animals, birds need food, water, shelter, and a mate if their species is going to survive. The change of seasons in some areas can alter a bird's habitat from a comfortable one with plenty of food, shelter, and water into one that is unsuitable. Most wild animals face the problem of living in a habitat that is only suitable part of the year. In order to survive, these animals must either migrate or hibernate. Since birds have the power of flight, most migrate; only a few species hibernate. Birds need to return to their nesting sites in the spring in order to reproduce.

Gearing Up

Birds need to prepare for the strenuous activity of migration. Birds are well-adapted for flight, but a bird needs a lot of fuel to propel it over hundreds of miles. Its internal biological clock is telling it to begin storing up fat for the first leg of its long journey. Its metabolism slows down, and it gains and stores the needed body fat under its skin. For a long-distance migrant, a good layover spot is essential for refueling its empty tank.

Patterns and Flyways

The patterns of migration are as diversified as the species that migrate. Some studies indicate that some birds use landmarks like rivers and mountains to guide them on their flight. Other birds use the earth's magnetic fields or the positions of the stars and sun to help them find their way. The best time to observe large numbers of birds migrating is in the spring months of April and May and in the fall months of September and October.

Flyways are routes birds take to accomplish their amazing journeys. Most birds that travel in or through the United States use one of four main flyways: Pacific, Central, Mississippi, and Atlantic. Many young birds learn the migratory route and favored layovers from the older adults.

Migration: *Instinctive Seasonal Movement of Animals (cont.)*

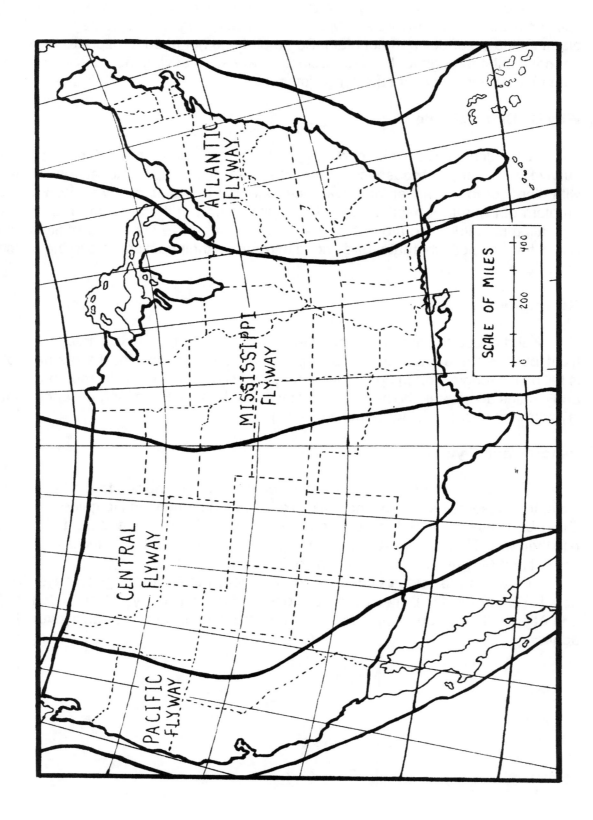

FLYWAYS OF THE UNITED STATES

Migration: *Instinctive Seasonal Movement of Animals (cont.)*

How High

Migrating altitudes vary with the species; however, most birds migrate at lower altitudes. Weather has the most influence on migrating altitudes. Most migratory birds fly under 15,000 feet above sea level. Bar-headed geese are the exception; they have been seen cresting above Mount Everest at an incredible 30,000 feet!

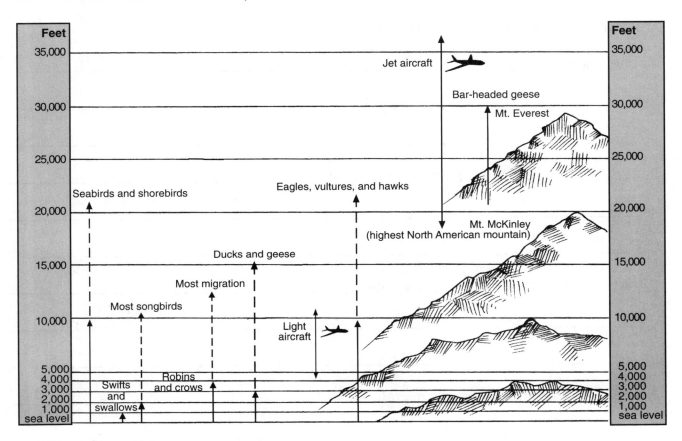

How Far and How Fast

Waterfowl (geese, ducks, and swans) cover hundreds of miles during a single flight. Most nest in the arctic region. Many shorebirds migrate 2,800 miles to South America. Seabirds, such as the arctic tern, travel from one end of the world to the other. They travel farther than any other bird. Many species of American land birds only migrate as far as the southern states.

Wind speed plays an important role in migration. As you might expect, different species of birds fly at different speeds. The wind can reach speeds of up to 20 miles per hour at migration altitudes. A strong head wind can stop a bird's forward progress or even send it backwards. Tail winds can easily double the bird's speed. A strong crosswind can cause a bird to fly far off-course, and this could result in a disastrous ending. Average airspeeds, without the influence of wind, range from 20 miles per hour for most songbirds to 40 miles per hour for larger shorebirds. Flight speed depends on the design of the bird's wings. Short, rounded wings normally fly between 15 and 25 miles an hour. Long, pointed wings enable some birds to fly at 40 or 50 miles an hour. Wings that sweep back like a jet can reach amazing speeds.

35

Name: _____ Date: _____

Migration: *Reinforcement Activity*

To the student observer: What is migration? _____

_____

Analyze: Which flyway do you live in? _____

Directions: Answer the following questions.

1. Why do birds migrate? _____

   _____

   _____

2. How do birds get ready for their long journey? _____

   _____

   _____

3. Where do birds go when they migrate? _____

   _____

   _____

4. How do birds find the correct migration path? _____

   _____

   _____

5. When is the best time to observe migration? _____

   _____

   _____

6. What are the four main flyways?

   a. _____   b. _____

   c. _____   d. _____

What Is Ecology?

Life can only exist in a very narrow zone, slightly above and below the surface of Earth, called the **biosphere**. The study of the relationships between living things and their environment is called **ecology**. The word *ecology* makes most people think of conservation efforts and recycling programs, but the true meaning is much broader. The word *ecology* comes from the Latin word *oikos,* which means "home."

Ecosystems

The living and nonliving parts of a specific environment make up an **ecosystem**. The nonliving parts include air, water, sunlight, and soil. All organisms need these things to survive. Ecosystems can be as large as an ocean or as small as a patch of brush behind your house.

Communities and Populations

Each ecosystem is made up of one or more **communities**. A community is all the organisms that live in a certain area. Community members are constantly interacting with one another and the nonliving parts of their environment. A change in one part of the ecosystem can cause a change in all parts. Each community is made up of **populations**. A population is all the members of one species that live in the same area. For example, all the frogs make up the frog population in the pond community. Can you think of some other populations in the pond community?

Biomes

The biosphere is divided into six major areas called **biomes**. Each biome has its own climate and supports various organisms that are well-adapted for living in each one. The six biomes are:
- **Tundra -** Bitterly cold and the ground remains frozen year round; very few plants and animals exist here
- **Coniferous Forest -** A cold climate made up of cone-bearing trees; home to many animals
- **Deciduous Forest -** A moderate climate of warm summers and cold winters made up of trees that shed their leaves in the fall; home to many animals
- **Tropical Rain Forest -** A warm and moist climate near the equator; supports more plant and animal species than any other biome
- **Grassland -** A moderate climate that supports mostly grasses but not trees; home to many grazing and burrowing animals
- **Desert -** An extremely dry climate with very little rainfall and poor soil; characterized by hot days and cold nights; home to only a few species of plants and animals

People and the Balance of Nature

The environment is always changing. These changes work together to help keep the environment in balance. If the environment is in balance, the community and size of populations remain **constant** (about the same). Sometimes the balance in an ecosystem is upset. People can upset the balance by destroying the **habitats** (homes of animals) or by polluting.

Name: _____ Date: _____

What Is Ecology?: *Reinforcement Activity*

To the student observer: An aquarium is an ecosystem you may have in your home. What does it mean if the aquarium is a healthy ecosystem?

_____

_____

Directions: Complete the following sentences below.

1. An ecosystem is made up of both _____ things.

2. The narrow zone of life is called the _____.

3. The study of relationships between the living and nonliving parts of an ecosystem is called

    _____.

4. The biosphere is divided into major areas called _____.

Matching (One will not be used.)

_____ 5. A hot dry area with few plants and animals.

_____ 6. A warm moist area with many kinds of plants and animals.

_____ 7. A moderate climate with many grasses and grazing animals.

_____ 8. A cold climate with cone-bearing trees and many animals.

_____ 9. A moderate climate with deciduous trees and many animals.

a. Tundra
b. Coniferous forest
c. Deciduous forest
d. Tropical rain forest
e. Grassland
f. Desert

Answer the questions below.

10. In which biome do you live? _____

    _____

11. Which biome supports the most life? _____

    _____

12. How can people upset the balance of nature? _____

    _____

    _____

    _____

Avian Endangerment Exhibit: *Research Project*

Extinction Is Forever

The number of bird species with declining populations is growing at an alarming rate. Many people today are trying to stop this trend. Let's research together to learn why their numbers are decreasing and what is being done to help these birds.

To the student observers: Draw a biome from your teacher's grab bag. Research to find out if there are any birds in that biome that are endangered or threatened. Select a bird whose population is declining to become a part of an "Avian Endangerment Exhibit."

Procedure:

1. Obtain a file folder from your teacher.

2. Place the name of the bird you are researching on the file tab.

3. Research to find the bird's habitat, diet, physical features, behavior, cause of decline, and the steps that are being taken to preserve it, along with any other interesting information you have found.

4. Use computer images, if available, magazine articles, or your own hand-drawn pictures for your endangered bird file.

5. Upon the completion of your research and project design, display your folder as part of your class's "Avian Endangerment Exhibit."

Name: _____ Date: _____

Bird Vocabulary: *Study Sheet*

To the student observer: This is a list of important terms used throughout the unit. Use this sheet to help you do the activities in the birds unit. You can also use this list of terms to help you study for the Unit Test.

1. **Adaptation** - a trait that helps an organism to survive in its environment.

2. **Archaeopteryx** - an ancient bird

3. **Aves** - the class of birds

4. **Classification** - to place into groups based on similarities

5. **Contour Feathers** - feathers used by a bird for flight

6. **Down Feathers** - feathers that provide warmth

7. **Ecology** - the study of the relationships between organisms and their environments

8. **Endothermic** - warm-blooded; able to maintain a constant temperature

9. **Extinction** - the end of a species

10. **Habitat** - where an organism lives

11. **Incubate** - female sitting on eggs to keep them warm

12. **Instinct** - an inborn behavior, such as nest building in birds

13. **Migration** - a seasonal movement of birds from one area to another

14. **Molt** - to shed worn out feathers

15. **Navigate** - to follow landmarks in order to find your way

16. **Ornithology** - the study of birds

17. **Plumage** - a bird's feathers

18. **Preening** - the process used by birds to waterproof their feathers

19. **Response** - a reaction to a change in the environment

20. **Stimulus** - something in the environment that causes a change in behavior

Name: _____ Date: _____

Birds: *Crossword Puzzle*

Directions: Use the information you have learned about birds to complete the puzzle below.

ACROSS

1. The natural home of an animal
4. Warm-blooded
10. A bird's feathers
11. Complex, innate behavior
12. The end of a species
15. An insulation feather
18. The earliest fossil known to have feathers
19. Seasonal movement from one area to another
20. The study of the relationship between living things and their environments

DOWN

2. The class of birds
3. A trait that helps an animal to survive in its environment
5. To follow landmarks in order to find your way
6. The study of birds
7. To shed and replace feathers
8. A flight feather
9. Process a bird uses to waterproof its feathers
13. Female sitting on eggs to keep them warm
14. To group organisms according to their similarities
16. Reaction of an organism to a stimulus
17. Something organisms respond to

Name: _____ Date: _____

Birds: *Unit Test*

Multiple Choice: Place the letter of the correct answer on the line beside each sentence.

_____ 1. Contour feathers
    a. act as an insulator.
    b. give birds their sleek shape.
    c. cover newly hatched birds.
    d. all of these.

_____ 2. Talons are
    a. hollow bones.
    b. special beaks.
    c. wings of penguins.
    d. sharp claws.

_____ 3. Migration is
    a. seasonal movement.
    b. a form of hibernation.
    c. bright colors for attracting a mate.
    d. establishing a territory.

_____ 4. A habitat is
    a. a bird's range.
    b. a bird's flyway.
    c. an area where a bird lives.
    d. a method of obtaining food.

_____ 5. A bird is
    a. a vertebrate.
    b. endothermic.
    c. an animal with feathers.
    d. all of these.

_____ 6. Birds do not have
    a. strong feathers.
    b. hollow bones.
    c. specialized beaks.
    d. beaks with teeth.

_____ 7. Fossils suggest birds may have come from
    a. reptiles.
    b. mammals.
    c. amphibians.
    d fish.

_____ 8. Birds lay
    a. amniotic eggs.
    b. leathery eggs.
    c. spotted eggs.
    d. eggs without shells.

_____ 9. Birds belong to class
    a. *Insecta.*
    b. *Ornithology.*
    c. *Reptilia.*
    d. *Aves.*

_____ 10. Most of a bird's body is taken up by
    a. huge muscles.
    b. air sacs.
    c. light bones.
    d. a complex digestive system.

Name: _____ Date: _____

Birds: *Unit Test (cont.)*

Short Answer: Answer the following questions.

11. How are a bird's wings designed for flight? _____
_____
_____

12. What is the strongest muscle in a bird's body and why? _____
_____
_____

13. If you eat very little, people say you eat like a bird. Why is this inaccurate? _____
_____
_____

14. List the adaptations that enable birds to fly. _____
_____
_____

15. State the four functions of feathers. _____
_____
_____

16. What are the five main groups of birds, classified by beaks and feet? _____
_____
_____

17. Name two examples of flightless birds. _____

Matching: Place the letter of the correct term on the line next to the corresponding definition.

_____ 18. Shedding old feathers   a. Ecology

_____ 19. Blending with the environment   b. Biosphere

_____ 20. Protecting feathers from rain   c. Preening

_____ 21. A fixed route used by migratory birds   d. Flyway

_____ 22. The study of relationships of living things and their environments   e. Ecosystem

_____ 23. The living and nonliving parts of an environment   f. Camouflage

_____ 24. The narrow zone of life   g. Molting

_____ 25. The end of a species   h. Extinction

Answer Keys

What Are Birds?: Reinforcement Activity (p. 3)
To the student observer: Answers will vary.
No, some birds do not fly.
Analyze: Webbed feet would be a disadvantage because the birds need feet to grab their prey.

1. **Puzzle**
   <u>B</u>eaks
   B<u>i</u>rd
   Wa<u>r</u>m-blooded
   Evi<u>d</u>ence
   Wing<u>s</u>

Questions
2. Light, hollow bones and wings with feathers.
3. reptiles
4. reptiles, mammals
5. Aves
6. a. Warm-blooded vertebrates
   b. Wings and feathers
   c. Hollow bones
   d. Beaks or bills without teeth
   e. Lay eggs with a hard shell

The History of Birds: Reinforcement Activity (p. 5)
To the student observer: Yes, birds are the only animals with feathers and hollow bones. Most birds fly and all are warm-blooded.
Analyze: They are softer and more fragile, so they decay more quickly.
1. Hollow bones and feathers
2. The study of birds
3. Class *Aves*
4. An early fossil known as archaeopteryx had several reptilian features but was similar to the birds we know today. For example, it had feathers.
5. People who study fossils
6. Toothed jaw, head with scales, claws, and a bony tail

Birds, Inside-Out: Reinforcement Activity (p. 8)
To the student observer: For flying and warmth
Analyze: They have scales on their feet and legs.
1. The bones are hollow and fused for strength so they don't add extra weight.
2. The wings are curved from front to back, creating lift.
3. The chest or pectoral muscles
4. Air sacs. They make the bird lighter.
5. The huge eye sockets and toothless beak reduce the weight of the skull.

Fly, Fly Away: Reinforcement Activity (p. 11)
To the student observer: A bird has a shoulder, an upper arm and elbow, a lower arm and wrist, and a hand with fingers and a thumb.
1. **Wings:** A bird has a curved shape that allows air to flow faster above the wing than below it. This causes a difference in air speed and lifts the bird.
2. **Body:** A bird's body is small and compact with a contoured shape. The bones are strong, hollow, and fused together. Much of the body is filled with air sacs.
3. **Feathers:** Are strong, flexible, and lightweight. A bird has three types of feathers that lie flat so air slides over them. Even their ears are covered by feathers. The long primaries are the flight feathers.
4. **Muscles:** Birds have large flight muscles. Twenty-five percent of a bird's body weight is flight muscle. They need large muscles to raise and lower their wings.
5. **Energy:** A bird has a lot of energy. Its circulatory and respiratory system keeps its energy level high and its weight low (a high metabolism rate). The digestive system is very fast, keeping the bird at a high level of energy.

Feathers and Flight: Reinforcement Activity (p. 14)
To the student observer: Feathers
1. a. Provide warmth
   b. Used in flight
   c. Waterproof the body
   d. Provide coloration for camouflage, attracting mates, and identification
2. a. Contour - outer feathers for flight
   b. Down - insulation for warmth
3. A protein called keratin, which gives feathers strength and flexibility
4. A. barbule   B. hook
   C. barb   D. shaft
   E. barb   F. shaft
   G. quill

Parts of a Feather: Student Lab Challenge (p. 15)
Observations:
6. Answers will vary. Accept any logical answers, "They go back together."
7. Crisscrossed inside with many air spaces.

Parts of a Feather: Student Lab Challenge (p. 16)
Conclusions:
1. The barbs and barbules of a contour feather make it airtight to give lift during flight.

2. The fluffy shape traps air close to the bird's body, producing a layer of insulation.
3. Because of its shape like a long pin
4. Answers will vary.
   A. contour - large, rigid shaft; barbs hooked together.
   B. down - smaller, fluffier, barbs not hooked, softer, flexible shaft.

Classification of Birds: Reinforcement Activity (p. 18)

To the student observer: To make it easier to study and communicate about things

Analyze: There are often too many common names for the same thing that could lead to communication errors among scientists.

1. They are arranged from general to the most specific relationship.
2. Taxonomy
3. The class level, because birds are the only animals with feathers.
4. The order level
5. The species level
6. Carolus Linnaeus
7. Binomial nomenclature
8. A. 3, B. 5, C. 4, D. 7, E. 2, F. 1, G. 6

Kinds of Birds: Reinforcement Activity (p. 23)

To the student observer: Because of their numbers and diversity

Analyze: They are grouped by body structure, beaks and feet, and behavior and song.

1. Birds of prey, perching birds, nonperching birds, wading birds, and swimming birds
2. Perching songbirds
3. Eagle
4. Penguins and ratites
5. They have reduced wings and flight muscles.

Matching

6. D	7. C	8. E
9. A	10. B	

Beaks and Feet: Investigating Bird Adaptations (p. 24)

Feet:

1. B	2. E	3. D
4. A	5. C	

Beaks and Feet: Investigating Bird Adaptations (p. 25)

Beaks:

1. C	2. B	3. A
4. D	5. F	6. G
7. E		

Who's Who: Classification Activity (p. 26)

A. bird of prey	B. swimming bird
C. wading bird	D. bird of prey
E. nonperching bird	F. flightless bird
G. perching bird	H. flightless bird

Owl Pellets: Lab Activity (p. 28)

Answers will vary.
1. Owl pellets are small clumps of organic material.
2. Skulls and jawbones
3. Yes, the smaller bones were crushed and digested.
4. Small rodents, such as shrews, mice, moles, and rats; these are the bones found most often.
5. Their digestive juices are not strong enough to dissolve the hard tissue.
6. Possible answers: keen eyesight, sharp talons, and curved beaks

The Behaviors of Birds: Reinforcement Activity (p. 32)

To the student observer: The way an organism responds to stimuli

Analyze: Answers will vary. Heat, cold, noise, etc.

1. Anything in the environment that causes a response or change in behavior
2. Innate—inborn; acquired—learned
3. Reflex acts and instincts

4. F	5. B	6. A
7. D	8. H	9. G
10. C	11. E	

Migration: Reinforcement Activity (p. 36)

To the student observer: The seasonal movement from one area to another

Analyze: Answers will vary. Teacher check.

1. To find a more comfortable habitat as the seasons change
2. They store up fat under their skin as their metabolism slows down.
3. They travel along a fixed route or flyway to their nesting site or their winter habitats.
4. Landmarks, position of stars and the sun, the earth's magnetic fields
5. Fall (September–October); spring (April–May)
6. a. Pacific   b. Central
   c. Mississippi   d. Atlantic

What is Ecology?: Reinforcement Activity (p. 38)

To the student observer: Population numbers stay the same. All the organisms receive the things they need to survive.

1. living and nonliving	2. biosphere
3. ecology	4. biomes
5. f 6. d	7. e

8. b   9. c   10. Teacher check.
11. Tropical rain forest
12. Pollution and destroying habitats

Birds: Crossword Puzzle (p. 41)

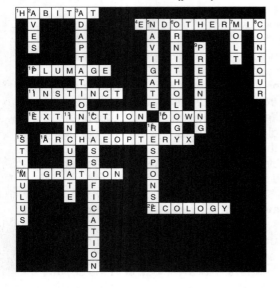

Birds: Unit Test (p. 42–43)

1. b	2. d	3. a
4. c	5. d	6. d
7. a	8. a	9. d
10. b		

11. They are curved from front to back, creating lift.
12. The pectoral or chest muscle is the strongest because it is used to operate the wings.
13. Birds eat a lot. They need constant energy to maintain flight.
14. Hollow bones, feathers, and specialized wings
15. Warmth, flight, waterproofing, coloration
16. Birds of prey, perching birds, nonperching birds, wading birds, and swimming birds
17. The ostrich, penguin, emu, rhea, cassowary, and kiwi (any two)

18. g	19. f	20. c
21. d	22. a	23. e
24. b	25. h	

Bibliography

Baily, Jim. *Birds of Prey.* New York: Facts on File Publication, 1988.

Daniel, Ortleb, Biggs. *Glencoe Life Science.* Columbus, Ohio: Glencoe/McGraw-Hill, 1997.

Freedman, Russell. *How Birds Fly.* New York: Holiday House, 1977.

Grange, Francois de la and Antoine Reille. *Birds, Science and Its Secrets.* Milwaukee: Raintree Publishers, 1988.

Hylander, Clarence. *Feathers and Flight.* New York: The Macmillan Company, 1959.

Lemmon, Robert S. *All About Birds.* New York: Random House, Inc., 1955.

Peterson, Roger, Tory. *The Birds, Life Nature Library.* New York: Time-Life, Inc., 1963.